For

THAT SPECIAL

You

Feeling Good About Yourself

By Dr. Rita Freedman

Design by Deborah Michel

Illustrations by Grace De Vito

PETER PAUPER PRESS, INC.
WHITE PLAINS · NEW YORK

To Stan — my special man

Copyright © 1994, 1996
Peter Pauper Press, Inc.
202 Mamaroneck Avenue
White Plains, NY 10601
ISBN 0-88088-867-9
Printed in Singapore
7 6 5 4

Contents

THAT *Special* YOU

I once asked a friend whether she had enjoyed her vacation abroad. *The trip was terrific,* she replied, *but unfortunately I had to take myself along.* Like it or not, you're stuck with your own self as a constant companion on life's journey.

How do you feel about the self that travels along with you? What words would you choose to describe its distinctive qualities? Curious? Friendly? Honest?

You carry your self-image everywhere you go, and it serves like a camera lens that filters all your experiences. For we don't see the world as it really is, but always in terms of who we are. And it makes a world of difference whether you view life's

5

voyage through a dark lens of self-regret or through a bright lens of self-respect.

This book explores many parts of the self that make up that special you. In it you'll find new ways to look at and laugh at yourself. I hope you'll also uncover some hidden dimensions of the self and welcome them as they emerge.

Seeing yourself as special doesn't depend on being young or smart, healthy or wealthy. Feeling good about yourself doesn't depend on what you say or what you weigh. You probably know people who have lots of good fortune, but still are plagued with self-doubt. And surely you've met others burdened with problems who still seem filled with self-confidence.

It isn't what you have or what you do, but how you react to who you are that causes the greatest pleasure or pain. Shakespeare observed that *nothing in the world is good or bad but thinking makes it so.* And this includes yourself. Since self-esteem is merely a state of mind, you *are* special, as long as you believe it.

As a clinical psychologist, I'm continually amazed at the diversity of human nature. No two of us are alike. Each self is exceptional, simply because it's unique: a one-of-a-kind truly singular sensation. Your own rare combination of qualities is interwoven like an elegant quilt with many intricate pieces arranged in a perfect pattern.

I hope that the ideas, facts, and quotations that follow will inspire you as you stitch together your personal self-quilt. Take time to wrap it around you and enjoy the warmth of its security. Then stand back to admire its unique design, as you proudly display that special you.

R. F.

The ESTEEMED You

Here's to you—just the way you are.
Come celebrate that sweet embraceable
*   you,*
A self worthy of high esteem.
A self deserving the same respect
*   you easily give to others.*
Here's to your flaws, your fears, your
*   many faults.*
Here's to your past:
*   who you were, where you've been,*
*   what you've done.*
Honoring who you are today is the first
*   step toward becoming all you can be*
*   someday.*

⊰Did you know?⊱

People with high self-esteem tend to have more
positive feelings about their bodies and about
other people as well. Having high self-esteem
doesn't protect you from self-doubt, but it does
allow you to feel unsure of yourself without
losing self-respect.

My motto is the same as my blood type:
B Positive.

Cynthia Nelms

❖

When I'm good, I'm very good. When I'm bad,
I'm better.

Mae West

❖

I realize I was brought up to be the person
others wanted me to be, so that they would like
me and not be bothered by my presence.

Liv Ullmann

❖

If one undervalues oneself, one naturally undervalues one's emotions: *Be happy? You mean me?
That's impossible. Anyway, how can it matter, if it's
only to do with me?*

Elizabeth Janeway

I began to understand that self-esteem isn't everything; it's just that there's nothing without it.

GLORIA STEINEM

⊷═◉═⊷

How many cares one loses when one decides not to be something but to be someone.

COCO CHANEL

⊷═◉═⊷

The more you challenge yourself, the more you learn to do, the more your self-esteem really shoots up: Hey! I can do this! You're a success.

MARY ANN GOFF

⊷═◉═⊷

To dream of the person you would like to be is to waste the person you are.

ANONYMOUS

The FEELING *You*

Feelings are a window on self-awareness.
They offer a glimpse of the hidden you.
Feelings can smolder or suddenly flare up,
exposing the dark side of the self.
This is why we try so hard to hide the envy, or veil the rage behind a smile.
What a challenge it is to own your emotions and know what to do with them!
Knowing when to share your fears, and when to spill your tears.

⇒ Did you know? ⇐

Strong emotions cause physical changes throughout the body. This is why feelings and thoughts are a two-way process. What the brain tells the body depends on what the body is telling the brain.

People who keep stiff upper lips find that it's damn hard to smile.

JUDITH GUEST

For too long the signs of our pleasure — smiling and laughing — have been used to make others feel better rather than used as a way to let others know how we feel.

REGINA BARRECA

The ability to feel is indivisible. Repress awareness of any one feeling, and all feelings are dulled.... The same nerve endings are required for weeping and dancing, fear and ecstasy.

SAM KEEN

If one is not permitted to express anger or even to recognize it within oneself, one is, by simple extension, refused both power and control.

CAROLYN HEILBRUN

15

Once in a while you have to take a break and visit yourself.

AUDREY GIORGI

It's important to own who you are. You're not all good and you're not all bad, but the owning is part of the passage, I think.

JUDY COLLINS

Those who do not know how to weep with their whole heart don't know how to laugh either.

GOLDA MEIR

15

The FRIENDLY *You*

*By being a friend, you befriend
   yourself.
We're each born a separate self, yet
   attached;
Alone, yet needing others.
Companions come in numerous colors.
Workmates and playmates, nearest
   neighbors and dearest chums.
Life washes friends in like shells on a
   beach.
Take time to gather them up and
   treasure your rare collection.*

⇛Did you know?⇚

People report that friends are less judgmental
than relatives; therefore they often find it easier
to share important parts of the self with friends.

Being a separate self is a most glorious, most lonely proposition. Loving oneself is nice but . . . incomplete.

JUDITH VIORST

What I cannot love, I overlook. Is that real friendship?

ANAÏS NIN

The more I traveled the more I realized that fear makes strangers of people who should be friends.

SHIRLEY MACLAINE

Friendship with oneself is all-important, because without it one cannot be friends with anyone else in the world.

ELEANOR ROOSEVELT

The STRIVING *You*

To strive is to feel more fully alive.
Each day challenges you to reach
 beyond the familiar into the
 unknown.
The greatest pleasure of striving lies
 not in the final product but in the
 daily process.
Stop a moment. Consider where you've
 come from, and where you still want
 to go.
Your goals need constant revision, as
 yesterday's hope gives way to today's
 reality, which in turn reshapes
 tomorrow's dreams.

⇹ Did you know? ⇷

While men strive for mastery mainly for its own
sake, women see mastery as a way of developing
relationships and gaining approval.

It is never too late to be what you might have been.

GEORGE ELIOT

✦══◉══✦

Opportunities are usually disguised as hard work, so most people don't recognize them.

ANN LANDERS

✦══◉══✦

Everything works better when you're working.

LAUREN BACALL

✦══◉══✦

Do what terrifies you. Everything else is boring.

LOIS GERACI ERNST

The JOYOUS You

*Joy isn't just contagious. It's also
  therapeutic, a healing antidote to
  ailments, mental and physical.*
*So remember to take your daily dose of
  nonsense, like a vitamin pill.*
*Cultivate your silly self, letting her
  bubble up from the dry well of your
  pain.*
*And savor the sound of your own
  laughter.*

⊰ Did you know? ⊱

When people are asked to perform tasks that
make them smile, they wind up actually feeling
happier.

For most women, humor is something we aren't sure how to use, because we've been told it's something we haven't got.

REGINA BARRECA

✦═◉═✦

A day during which we have laughed is a day that has not been wasted.

REGINA BARRECA

✦═◉═✦

You grow up the day you have your first real laugh—at yourself.

ETHEL BARRYMORE

✦═◉═✦

Laughter is like the human body wagging its tail.

ANNE WILSON SCHAEF

21

The SADDENED You

You greeted life with a heartfelt cry,
and your seasonal tears are as
natural as spring rain.
They're the price of admission to life's
garden.
As you gather your daily bouquet of
experience, you'll find lots of thorns
between the roses, lots of weeds
among the lilies.
Just mix the sad taste of your tears
with the sweet smell of those
blossoms.

⊰ Did you know? ⊱

At every age, women suffer higher rates of
depression than men, perhaps because women
have a greater tendency to blame themselves
when things go wrong.

If you want a place in the sun, prepare to put up with a few blisters.

ABIGAIL VAN BUREN

The world is round and the place which may seem like the end may also be only the beginning.

IVY BAKER PRIEST

You can't be brave if you've only had wonderful things happen to you.

MARY TYLER MOORE

Sometimes the only thing left to hang onto is letting go.

LINDA MOAKES

The GUILTY You

Guilt is the enemy of self-esteem.
It's the critical voice of self-abuse that
blames you for who you are, then
shames you for who you're not.
Of course, your faults only confirm your
humanity.
So silence the chorus of guilt by raising
the voice of forgiveness.
Find compassion for the real you and
stop demanding a perfect ideal.

⊰Did you know?⊱

In the short term people tend to regret things
they've done. But, in the long term, they regret
the things they didn't do.

As perfectionists we ensure that we will never be satisfied… A search for perfection is always a search for fault.

Susan Kano

⇢═◯═⇠

Experience [is] the name we give to our mistakes.

Harriet Goldhor Lerner

⇢═◯═⇠

Being loved anyway is not being regarded as perfect but being accepted as imperfect.

Ellen Goodman

⇢═◯═⇠

Women keep a special corner of their hearts for sins they have never committed.

Cornelia Otis Skinner

The CURIOUS You

*Curiosity makes each moment
    remarkable.*
*Remember when learning was your
    main activity?*
*Kids work nonstop to make sense out of
    nonsense.*
*In a game of mental gymnastics they
    ponder and explore, meditate, and
    contemplate the extraordinary
    aspects of ordinary things.*
*If you could only recapture that
    childish wonder and regain the
    rapture of a toddler with a new toy!*
*Life can have greater meaning if you
    keep on looking for meaning in life.*

⊰ Did you know? ⊱

Babies have a natural curiosity to explore the
world for the sheer pleasure of doing it. We
learn more in the first year of our lives than at
any other time.

I could not, at any age, be content to take my place in a corner by the fireside and simply look on. Life was meant to be lived. Curiosity must be kept alive.

ELEANOR ROOSEVELT

That's what learning is. You suddenly understand something you've understood all your life, but in a new way.

DORIS LESSING

You know, when you're young and curious, people love to teach you.

DEDE ALLEN

Ignorance is no excuse, it's the real thing.

IRENE PETER

The HEALTHY You

*Minding your body really matters, for
the body is a house that shelters the
self.*

*Weathered by time and neglect,
battered by illness and trauma, your
house needs daily maintenance and
repair.*

*Certain parts are always breaking
down, while others are healing up.*

Illness and wellness are relative states.

*So if you're sick of feeling sick,
remember that YOU are not your
illness.*

*You can reach for recovery by restoring
harmony between mind and body,
between spirit and nature.*

⁂ Did you know? ⁂

The majority of visits to doctors are for illnesses
that will ultimately get better by themselves.

If you look at what the disease means to you, it may help you make changes in your life that help you heal.

BERNIE SIEGEL

I think of my illness [ovarian cancer] as a school, and finally I've graduated.

GILDA RADNER

Health is not a condition of matter, but of Mind.

MARY BAKER EDDY

Happiness is good health and a bad memory.

INGRID BERGMAN

The PRESSURED *You*

Stress: a contagious disease that spreads when demands exceed available time.

Are you caught in a cycle of stress?

Are you driven by internal deadlines and impossible shoulds?

Pressured by too many choices, too much control?

Stress leads to distress—exhaustion, burnout, breakdowns and breakups.

We get so overworked and overbooked, we overlook our need for rest and relaxation.

Try giving yourself permission, for one whole day, to simply do nothing.

⇥ Did you know? ⇤

Doctors believe that the vast majority of all illnesses are either triggered by or sustained by stress.

When my kids become wild and unruly, I use a nice, safe playpen. When they're finished, I climb out.

Erma Bombeck

⊷══◯══⊶

For fast-acting relief, try slowing down.

Jane Wagner

⊷══◯══⊶

The art of life is not controlling what happens to us, but *using* what happens to us.

Gloria Steinem

⊷══◯══⊶

The direction of our lives is more important than the speed at which we travel them.

Harriet Goldhor Lerner

31

The LOVING *You*

Love is the pulse of life.
Hold out your heart and offer it up.
Only by giving your love away can you
    make room for the heartbeat of
    another.
Be brave enough to drop the
    boundaries and lift the barriers.
Then a great stream of passion can
    flow in.
Who knows where the tides of love will
    carry you?

⊰ Did you know? ⊱

Men fall in love faster than women and are
governed more by their romantic feelings.
Women tend to be more practical and restrained
by their need for a suitable mate.

Love doesn't just sit there, like a stone, it has to be made, like bread; re-made all the time, made new.

URSULA K. LEGUIN

Don't be too choosy or stingy about whom or how often you love.

HELEN GURLEY BROWN

The giving of love is an education in itself.

ELEANOR ROOSEVELT

You need someone to love you while you're looking for someone to love.

SHELAGH DELANEY

The SENSUOUS *You*

Come fill up your senses...become a
  sensuous woman.
One who nurtures her physical
  appetites by dancing, playing,
  hugging, touching and tasting all the
  delicious parts of life.
A sensuous woman tunes in to her
  body, turning it on rather than tuning
  it out.
Self-love grows from bodylove, and
  bodylove grows from sensuality.

⊰Did you know?⊱

People who care about fitness and health have
more positive feelings about their bodies than
those who care primarily about their looks.

Why not fall in love with the body you've been
sleeping with all your life?

STEWART EMERY

Coming of age with dignity means looking as
mature as we really are and still seeing ourselves
as sensuous human beings.

RITA FREEDMAN

I try to have one terrific smell every day. I like to
give my nose a snack.

JANE WAGNER

To achieve bodylove you must strike a balance
between your ornamental needs for adornment,
your instrumental needs for achievement, and
your sensual needs for fulfillment.

RITA FREEDMAN

The GROWING You

Growth demands change…and loss.
To greet the future you must move
beyond the past and accept the
necessary losses.
Growing up means letting go, giving
in, moving on.
It means shedding your old familiar
skin to try out new roles and to
travel new roads.
Right now, at this very moment, you
ARE who you are becoming.

⇥ Did you know? ⇤

For most girls and women, the challenge of
growing up means figuring out how to become
separate individuals while still staying connected
to loved ones.

It has begun to occur to me that life is a stage I'm going through.

ELLEN GOODMAN

Those who spend their lives in closets smell of mothballs.

MUGSY PEABODY

The past was full of surprises; the present is astonishing (as well as frightening); who knows what the future may be?

ELIZABETH JANEWAY

I love my past. I love my present. I'm not ashamed of what I've had, and I'm not sad because I have it no longer.

COLETTE

The purpose of living is to get old enough to have something to say.

M. F. K. Fisher

⊷═◉═⊶

The toughest role is learning to grow up.

Elizabeth Taylor

⊷═◉═⊶

Growth itself contains the germ of happiness.

Pearl S. Buck

⊷═◉═⊶

The strongest principle of growth lies in human choice.

George Eliot

The HUNGRY *You*

With food we feed our hungry hearts.
This is a basic truth you learned long
    ago: that milk and cookies = Mom =
    joy = love.
Do you still relish the hearty appetites
    of your childhood?
Or are you caught, like so many women,
    in a slender trap where fearing food
    and fighting fat are a way of life?
Only if you shed the diet mentality can
    hunger help preserve your health.
Through your love of food, you can
    nourish your love of self.

⊱ Did you know? ⊰

On any given day, 2/3 of high school girls and
1/3 of adult women report that they are dieting.
Four women out of five feel too heavy and want
to lose weight.

Never eat more than you can lift.

Miss Piggy

My idea of heaven is a great big baked potato and someone to share it with.

Oprah Winfrey

The sense of fullness and swelling, of curves and softness, of the awareness of plenitude and abundance which filled me with disgust and alarm, were actually the qualities of a woman's body.

Kim Chernin

If you can't have your piece of the cake, collect all the crumbs you can find.

Hattie Rosenthal

The COURAGEOUS You

Courageous acts are commonplace.
We're surrounded by staunch survivors
of illness and abuse.
By brave Moms who stand firm and
bold friends who walk tall.
Who are the heroic figures in your life?
Watch them as they face trauma,
overcome cowardice and defy
convention.
These role models can encourage you to
break free of your own crippling
fears,
To take risks and fight on against great
odds.

⇝ Did you know? ⇜

Women need special courage because they must
often live the final years of their lives without
partners. The average age of widowhood is close
to 60.

I say to you what I say to myself every morning: go out and live like warriors! The coward's life is not worth living.

ERICA JONG

❖⟫❡⟪❖

The most courageous act is still to think for yourself. Aloud.

COCO CHANEL

❖⟫❡⟪❖

Life shrinks or expands according to one's courage.

ANAÏS NIN

❖⟫❡⟪❖

You have to accept whatever comes and the only important thing is that you meet it with courage and with the best that you have to give.

ELEANOR ROOSEVELT

The DIVIDED *You*

The self gets divided by a complex
  world.
Are you burdened by multiple roles?
Are there too many parts of you
    pulling in different directions, all
    needing to be heard at once?
As you shift roles from worker to
    mother to lover to friend...
    focus on a balancing point where
    your many selves merge,
    and where YOU can emerge with
    integrity.

⊰Did you know?⊱

Three out of four women with children under 17
work both inside and outside the home. Working
mothers still do 70% of household chores.

If I can't have it all, can I at least have some of yours?

RITA RUDNER

❖─═❍═─❖

[I'm just like] every woman who gets up in the morning and gets breakfast for her family and goes off to a job . . . where she assumes a different role for the hours she's at work, who runs out at lunch to buy material for a costume for her daughter or to buy invitations for a party.... Our lives are a mixture of these different roles.

HILLARY RODHAM CLINTON

❖─═❍═─❖

One of the worst irritations in life is the fact that by the time you get it all together, you're too old to lift it.

MARY MARTIN

Being a woman is in itself a full-time job. On top of her job, a woman has to take care of children, take care of the household and take care of the man. And then she also has to try to look thirty-six for her entire life. No one can do that—most American women have a life that it would take six people to lead.

Fran Lebowitz

＊━◯━＊

Women are trained to speak softly...and carry a lip-stick.

Bella Abzug

＊━◯━＊

[Motherhood is regarded as] an extracurricular activity [for a woman] in addition to her career.

Judith D. Schwartz

47

The HONEST You

To thine own self be true.
It sounds so easy.
Yet honesty can often be complicated,
*   and also feel threatening.*
Fear underlies most lies.
That's why we hide truth, using self-
*   deception for self-protection.*
Can you trust yourself enough to stop
*   pretending?*
Can you find the courage to face up to
*   reality?*
Being true to yourself allows you to
*   share truth with others.*

⚜ Did you know? ⚜

Most women admit that at some time they have
lied about their age. Deception is a part of
everyday life, as we pretend to be younger,
blonder or rosier than we really are.

Lying is done with words and also with silence.

ADRIENNE RICH

Affirmations? That's where you lie to yourself until it's true.

LINDA MOAKES

The truth is the funniest thing around.

KAREN RIPLEY

Pretending is potentially the most serious form of deception because it can involve *living* a lie, rather than telling one.

HARRIET GOLDHOR LERNER

The LOVELY You

*Looking lovely depends on how well
  you do the looking.
It's time to study your face with loving
  eyes, and behold the beauty that's
  beyond the mirrored image.
Too many of us wind up looking good,
  but still feeling bad about our looks.
Perhaps it's time to start making over
  your mind instead of your face or
  your body.
You have a right to enjoy your own
  unique features, a right to feel
  comfortable in your own skin.*

⊰ Did you know? ⊱

Most women feel self-conscious about their
appearance and one out of four reports feeling
self-conscious all the time.

For many women, the body appears to grow beautiful and erotic as they grow to like the person in it.

Naomi Wolf

↔══○══↔

Here's my morning ritual. I open a sleepy eye, take one horrified look at my reflection in the mirror and then repeat with conviction, *I'm me and I'm wonderful. Because God doesn't make junk.*

Erma Bombeck

↔══○══↔

Not until women stop suffering for beauty will they stop suffering, too, for the lack of it.

Wendy Kaminer

↔══○══↔

Loss of beauty is one of the hazards of having it.

Rita Freedman

The RESTING You

Remember the Sabbath and keep it
   holy.
*This ancient commandment reminds
   you to make time for spiritual rest
   and renewal.*
*Time to retreat from daily cares and
   reclaim a peaceful place where you
   can simply BE in the here and now.*
*There, in the solitude of self-reflection,
   there, in the serenity of silence, you
   may hear the secrets that your soul
   reveals.*

⊰ Did you know? ⊱

Our bodies are preprogrammed to rest on a 24-
hour cycle. Sleeping and dreaming are so basic
to life that animals don't survive if they are
constantly kept awake.

No day is so bad it can't be fixed with a nap.

CARRIE SNOW

If six days a week I'm responsible
And self-sufficient and competent and
    mature,
On the seventh could I go find a womb
    to return to?

JUDITH VIORST

Never am I less alone than when I am by myself,
never am I more active than when I do nothing.

CATO

Inside myself is a place where I live all alone,
and that's where you renew your springs that
never dry up.

PEARL S. BUCK

The POWERFUL You

Power is part of every relationship.
Have you learned to seek power
 ·assertively?
Can you use it confidently—to act as
    well as attract, to make choices as
    well as changes, to influence decisions
    and to implement them?
When you combine inner strength with
    outer assets you gain a vital tool for
    helping and for healing.
Don't be afraid to freely use your
    power, not to dominate others but to
    empower them.

⊰ Did you know? ⊱

Analysis of media images indicates that men
generally are portrayed as active, dominant, and
strong, while women are shown as attractive,
submissive, and weak.

Many women have more power than they recognize, and they're very hesitant to use it, for they fear they won't be loved.

Patricia Schroeder

The hand that rocks the cradle rules the world.

Old Saying

If you lead a country like Britain...you have to have a touch of iron about you.

Margaret Thatcher

One can never consent to creep when one feels the impulse to soar.

Helen Keller

As females expand their power base beyond the powder room, one of their greatest challenges will be to resist the masculine goal of one-upmanship, a goal that can feel as ill-fitting to a woman as a man-tailored suit.

RITA FREEDMAN

The thing women must do to rise to power is redefine their femininity. Once, power was considered a masculine attribute. In fact, power has no gender.

EVELYN BEILENSON